RECRUIT YOURSELF

EARN A NCAA FOOTBALL SCHOLARSHIP

MICKEY DOLLENS

outskirtspress

DENVER, COLORADO

Outskirts Press, Inc.
http://www.outskirtspress.com

ISBN: 978-1-4327-9934-2

Outskirts Press and the "OP" logo are trademarks belonging to Outskirts Press, Inc.

PRINTED IN THE UNITED STATES OF AMERICA

This book is dedicated to my younger brother,
Joseph Dollens -
a champion of the underdog

April 2, 1992 – January 22, 2011

Dear Haase family,

I'm glad we've been close throughout the my whole life. Thank you for all the love and support.

Love,
Mikey 10-4-13

TABLE OF CONTENTS

ACKNOWLEDGEMENTS

There are many people to thank – I simply cannot list all of those who have helped me and influenced my life. But I would like to acknowledge and give special thanks to those people who have helped and influenced me throughout my high school football career and encouraged me in writing this particular book.

First of all, I'd like to thank my parents Steve and Connie Dollens. You taught me to value myself and to value others. You have taught me to be non-judgmental and to follow my own path. You have shared your thoughts and always let me make up my own mind. Thank you. I love you both very much.

I also must acknowledge those who have inspired me throughout my journey to earning a football scholarship: Family, friends, teachers, teammates, and high school coaches. Each of you impacted my life in a unique way. Thank you for the encouragement, challenges, and sharing your wisdom.

I wish to thank Magz, Nathan Boutwell, and Red Pencil Editing for your helpful advice and editing critiques.

Finally, I would like to thank . . . you, the reader for taking time to read and examine my strategies for earning a coveted football scholarship. I hope that my book will inform you on the football recruiting process, enhance your scholarship endeavors, and prove useful to life beyond football.

DON'T LEAVE YOUR COMPETITIVE SPIRIT ON THE FOOTBALL FIELD

You are a competitor. The moment you put on a helmet, you begin unleashing your competitive spirit. While competing on the football field was initially your athletic goal, you have had to vie for a position on the team first, and then continually compete to *keep* your starting position.

You'll probably never forget the challenge, as you struggle to balance an intensive training schedule along with long hours of studying, keeping your mind and body physically fit. But when you take to the football field each week to face your opponents, you are filled with an indescribable sense of pride and accomplishment — you know that you have earned the right to be on the field. This achievement is a process that begins with determination and passion, which I discovered on my own journey of earning a NCAA football scholarship.

The phrase "to earn" is key — in any given year, about 250,000 high school athletes compete for approximately

5,000 football scholarships. As you begin your journey, don't be discouraged by these statistics or any other obstacles that may stand in your way. Just be every bit as competitive in your pursuit for a scholarship as you were in competing for a position on your high school team, and against its rivals each week.

For example, let's discuss "Player A." Player A is in the perfect situation to land a football scholarship — he's a standout player on a powerhouse team that is well-known for its winning tradition. Because of his school's reputation for graduating great athletes, his coach is well-connected with college coaches around the country. In any given season, a junior on that team will catch the eye of a coach from a major university, who will then recruit that player, offering him a full-ride scholarship. "Player B" is in a much different situation. Although he may be as talented as Player A, he attends a relatively unknown high school, lacking in football prestige. During his junior year, his team was 3-7, and his senior year, 1-9, resulting in the firing of his coach. Needless to say, Player B wasn't on the NCAA's radar.

Do you think Player B's situation is hopeless? Absolutely not. I know this because I was Player B. By successfully "recruiting" myself, I ultimately earned a full-ride football scholarship to Southern Methodist University, where I played for the SMU Mustangs from 2006 to 2011, including playing in the 2009 Hawaii Bowl and 2010 Armed Forces Bowl.

As athletes, we are all used to taking command of a game situation and turning it into our advantage. *Recruit Yourself* offers you the opportunity to direct your strategic thinking and competitive nature toward taking command of your scholarship potential — no matter how your high school team performs or what school you attend.

Winning is the measurement of accomplishing goals; however, the value of playing football goes far beyond gridiron success. Life is a competitive process. Whether you're applying for a job, seeking a promotion, or even dating, you're always competing to some degree. Much of your success in life will depend on your ability to highlight and present your best qualities. The *Recruit Yourself* philosophy will offer you strategies that extend far beyond high school and college.

If you're among the vast number of players who are athletically and academically qualified to play college football but lack the ability to market themselves, then this book can help you unlock that information.

In the following pages, I will show you how to use the power of social media to recruit yourself to college football coaches. I will provide valuable information on the NCAA scholarship structure and share insider tips and advice that I have accumulated throughout my experience as a high school and collegiate athlete.

As a freshman in high school, I set a goal of earning a NCAA scholarship. I wasn't really sure of what to expect during the recruiting process, and I kept asking myself, "Why hasn't someone who has actually earned a football scholarship written a step-by-step guide on how to successfully market oneself?" Well, now there is such a book, and it's been my pleasure to write it.

THE RECRUIT YOURSELF
GAME PLAN

You already know how much of a difference a strategic game plan can make on the playing field. Winning teams understand the importance of preparing for their opponents. A strategic game plan is even more vital to winning a NCAA football scholarship, because you aren't competing against one opponent; you're competing against tens of thousands of opponents.

The NCAA's definition of "recruiting" is "any solicitation of prospective student-athletes or their parents by an institutional staff member or by a representative of the institution's athletics interests for the purpose of securing a prospective student-athlete's enrollment and ultimate participation in the institution's intercollegiate athletics program." No matter how talented you are, don't expect college coaches and recruiters to call you on the phone or come knocking on your door. There are more than one million high school football players in the United States, and at least twenty-five percent of these aspire to play at the collegiate level. Because college recruiters can't possibly scout every high school in the entire country, thousands of talented players miss out on playing college football because they don't have a proactive approach when it comes to recruitment. Don't get lost in the shuffle.

A proactive approach involving strategic marketing will set you apart from your competition, and help you gain the attention of college coaches.

KNOW YOUR MARKET

- Become familiar with the NCAA scholarship process, NCAA Divisions, and colleges in each division.

- Identify colleges that fit your talents and situation best.

CREATE AN ATHLETE PROFILE

- Remember you're selling a product and that product is you. Since your athlete resume, cover letter, highlight video and academic records may be the only tangible communication that coaches have from you, consider them your own sales brochure.

TARGET YOUR MARKET

- Create an Advertising Campaign

KNOW YOUR MARKET: NCAA SCHOLARSHIPS

The National Collegiate Athletic Association (NCAA) is a non-profit organization with a membership consisting of more than 1,200 colleges and universities, conferences and other organizations. As the administrator for 23 sports and championships relating to those sports, NCAA enforces rules and regulations, and oversees the distribution of money to member institutions. While NCAA is synonymous with athletic scholarships, more scholarships are available in football than in any of the other collegiate sports.

For a football player, one of the main differences between each NCAA division is the availability of athletic scholarships and financial aid.

Most high school football players dream about playing for a major Division I university. But don't discount colleges in the other NCAA divisions. Discounting alternative NCAA divisions is one of the biggest mistakes you can make in marketing yourself because it limits your opportunities to only 20 percent of all scholarships available.

Be prepared to target 100 percent of your possibilities by balancing your marketing efforts between all divisions and optional programs that apply to you and your specific situation. Obtaining a football scholarship from any college is a monumental success.

Let's look at the different divisions within the NCAA and what they can offer you as a student-athlete:

NCAA Division I FBS (Football Bowl Series) is the premiere scholarship program, which makes 85 full-ride scholarships available per team. Each year, coaches in this division can award up to 25 new scholarships that exclude any scholarships they may take from some players and give to others. Although FBS offers more scholarships than any other division, it only accounts for 20 percent of the opportunities in collegiate football. Some of these universities need no introduction: Texas A&M, the University of Alabama, the University of Southern California, Notre Dame, and the University of Michigan. This division also includes some that are less well known, such as the University of North Texas and the University of Central Florida.

NCAA Division 1 FCS (Football Championship Series) schools award 63 scholarships, which may include full-ride and partial scholarships. Full-ride scholarships are typically based on player quality and position importance. While some athletes can qualify at the FBS level, they choose a FCS school because their chances of playing right away are greater. Just a few of the universities in this division include Appalachian State University, the Citadel, Eastern Kentucky University, and the ancient rivals Harvard and Yale.

NCAA Division II (D2) awards 36 scholarships per team. Coaches offer a combination of full-ride and partial scholarships. Be sure to include D2 schools in your target marketing. These teams are very competitive and a number of NFL athletes are drafted each year at the D2 level. Some of the universities in this division are West Virginia State University, Northern Michigan University, and Colorado State University in Pueblo.

NCAA Division III schools offer financial aid instead of athletic scholarships. But don't eliminate these schools from your target marketing efforts. A combination of financial aid options such as federal aid and merit scholarships can often equate to larger funding assistance than an athletic scholarship in a higher division. A few of these colleges are Birmingham-Southern, Framingham State, North Carolina Wesleyan, and Gettysburg College.

NAIA (National Association of Intercollegiate Athletics) offers up to 24 full football scholarships per team, which are typically divided into partial scholarships. NAIA oversees sporting programs for more than 300 college athletic departments. Although NAIA schools tend to be smaller than NCAA colleges, most compete at the level comparable to an average NCAA Division II Program. Since the majority of high school athletes and their parents are unaware of NAIA, you can have the recruitment advantage over athletes who don't know about

NAIA. Take a look at their website (www.naia.org) for a list of participating colleges.

NJCAA (National Junior College Athletic Association) is a perfect fit for some athletes who may not be academically eligible for a four-year college or who may need to mature athletically. Two-year junior colleges or community colleges offer an excellent opportunity to get a quality education and play college sports at an affordable price. NJCAA member schools in Division 1 and 2 can offer athletic scholarships. But NJCAA Division 3 schools do not offer athletic scholarships.

THE NCAA CLEARING HOUSE ELIGIBILITY CENTER

You must register with the NCAA Eligibility Center in order to receive clearance to play at the NCAA Division I and Division II levels. Go to their website at: http://web1.ncaa.org/ ECWR2/ NCAA_EMS/NCAA.jsp and set up your account at the beginning of your junior year. More than 180,000 high school athletes register annually. By getting in the system early, you can avoid the mad rush to get NCAA clearance at the end of the school year.

The purpose of registration is to determine your academic eligibility and amateur status. After you've completed a thorough application, your high school must submit your complete official transcript to the Eligibility Center. Your SAT or ACT testing center should likewise send your official test scores directly to the Eligibility Center. This process must be duplicated each time you take the SAT or ACT test. And your senior transcript must also be submitted and mailed to NCAA. The address for mailing these documents is The NCAA Eligibility Center – P.O. Box 7136, Indianapolis, IN, 46207.

THE NCAA NATIONAL LETTER OF INTENT (NLI)

A NLI is a contract that goes beyond any verbal agreement you may have with a college coach to play for his team. It's a written document between you and the school that essentially protects both parties.

By signing a NLI, you're making an official one-year commitment to a particular college or university in exchange for an athletic scholarship. Signing a NLI means that you have officially secured a football scholarship. National signing day takes place each year on the first Wednesday of February.

ACADEMICS

Don't count on earning a football scholarship based solely on your athletic ability. Athletic talent is only half of what coaches are seeking.

To put the scholarship process in perspective, college coaches have x-amount of scholarship dollars to award. They're going to spend those dollars wisely by recruiting athletes whose performance in the classroom rivals their performance on the playing field.

Therefore the more you increase your grade point average (GPA), the more you increase your recruitment potential. Coaches look for well-rounded high school athletes that have the potential to successfully transition into a college student-athlete.

The NCAA has specific requirements regarding an athlete's high school GPA and standardized test scores, such as the ACT and SAT. The higher your grades, the more interest you'll attract.

Your high school guidance counselor is vital to your pursuit of a NCAA scholarship. Though the rules for NCAA eligibility are ever changing – and often confusing – your counselor is knowledgeable on the ins and outs of university academic standards and qualifications. Begin meeting with your guidance counselor immediately_so he or she can get – and keep – you on track for complying with all regulations. For example, my guidance counselor was invaluable to my scholarship journey. As a result of her professional direction, I learned how to build my high school resume and use several ACT and SAT resources.

MARKETING ESSENTIALS

You would never consider stepping onto a football field to face an opposing team without the proper equipment: your helmet, pads, and cleats. Likewise, you cannot properly market yourself to prospective colleges without the proper equipment: your cover letter, athlete resume, and highlight video.

COVER LETTER

Your cover letter introduces you to coaches. This is your first chance to make a good impression. Therefore, your cover letter must be crafted with professionalism and should be checked for grammatical errors, typos or misspelled words. I suggest you ask someone such as your English teacher to review and edit your letter.

Keep your cover letter to one page and your message to the point. Since your athlete resume and highlight video will do most of the talking for you, use your cover letter to briefly introduce yourself, state the purpose of the letter and direct the coach to your attached athlete resume and highlight video. Here is a sample to help you structure your cover letter concisely:

- Personalized greeting: Dear Coach _____,

- Paragraph One. Introduce yourself and state the purpose of your letter:

- My name is Mickey Dollens. I am a junior (class of ____) at Bartlesville High School in Bartlesville, Oklahoma. I'm the starting varsity defensive end and offensive lineman for the Bruins. This letter is to accompany the highlight video as part of my recruitment evaluation for SMU Mustangs.

- Paragraph Two. Briefly mention your qualifications and personal characteristics that make you the right fit for their team:

- Throughout my high school career, I successfully navigated the challenges of the life of a student-athlete and consistently improve my performance on the field and in the classroom. I believe that my game statistics, leadership skills, and strong work ethic testify to my strong collegiate athlete potential and qualify me for further evaluation.

- Paragraph Three. Present links to your highlight video and online social media profiles:

- My athlete resume and highlight video are attached. I hope that you'll please review them and let me know if you would like any more information from me. I would be honored to have the opportunity to play for you, Coach _____.

Close your letter with:
Sincerely,
Your Name
Your Area Code and Phone Number
Your Email Address
Your High School Name and Address
The YouTube Link to Your Highlights Video

ATHLETE RESUME

When you market yourself to a prospective employer, the quality of your work resume can determine whether or not you'll receive further evaluation and an interview. The same is true when presenting your athlete resume to prospective coaches because you're basically applying for a position on a college football team. An athlete resume showcases your accomplishments in athletics, academics, and tells coaches who you are on and off the field. You can create your resume with Microsoft Word (.doc) or Adobe PDF (.pdf).

A properly, well-constructed resume can generate tremendous interest from coaches and recruiters. Similar to your cover letter, your athlete resume must be typed and grammatically correct.

Be honest. Credibility is part of the total package that coaches want. Don't be tempted to inflate your stats on the field because you "think" it will increase your value. That deceitful tactic will come back to haunt you. If a college coach suspects that you've provided exaggerated information, he'll either promptly discard your resume or verify the information with your high school coach. Either way, you'll destroy your chances of being successfully recruited.

Begin your resume by including the following information: Your Name; Graduating Year; Position On Offense/Defense; Date of Birth; Height/Weight; Jersey Number; Home Address; Area Code/Phone Number; Email Address; High School Name/Address/Phone Number; High School Conference; Head Coach's Name/Phone Number; and the Names/Phone Numbers of any other coaches such as your position coach.

In order to give a college coach a sense of familiarity, include a picture of yourself in the top right-hand corner of the page. Below that, create a section entitled *Athletic Achievements*. Under that heading, list any stats that are relevant to your position(s). For example: sacks, tackles, rushing yards/average per carry, passing attempts/completion, receptions, interceptions, etc. Include honors such as All-State, All-District, All-Conference, and Team Captain. List your most impressive stats first and put them on the first page so they will stand out. At a glance, a coach can readily see the qualities you can bring to his team. For example, subtle honors such as Team Captain show your leadership qualities.

Colleges want to see a well-rounded student. So complete your profile with a section titled *Academic Statistics*. Include the following information that applies to you: GPA, SAT/ACT Scores, Class Rank, noteworthy Academic Honors, Class Office (such as Junior Class President), Extracurricular School Activities, what you're interested in studying during college, and Community Services. (You do not have to list academic information such as SAT/ACT scores if you feel it does not help you).

HIGHLIGHT VIDEO

Producing a quality highlight video is one of the most important steps you'll take toward building your recruiting platform. The quality of your highlight video can make or break your chances of acquiring further scholarship evaluation. Each year, coaches receive hundreds of highlight videos and nothing will make them turn off a video faster than poor viewing quality.

Aside from viewing quality and ease, coaches look for specific things. A video provides coaches with a quick, effective medium to evaluate skill, ability, intelligence, and determination.

A quality highlight video is often your best shot as an unknown athlete to get on a coach's recruiting radar. You need to produce a quality highlight video that will get and keep a coach's attention. First, you need to acquire game film from previous varsity games in which you've played. Ideally, your high school coaches already incorporate the computer software Hudl, which makes it much easier for you and your coach to break down game film and create a quality highlight video. If your high school coaches do not use Hudl, inform them that you'll need to collect game footage in order to make a highlight video for college recruitment. Secondly, make sure your school shoots games with new film on a high quality camera. If your school dubs over old footage year after year, the viewing quality will be too poor for your highlight video.

Here are a few steps you can take to make sure your highlight video gets viewed by coaches and makes a lasting impression. Your goal here is two-fold: (1) to produce a video that coaches watch and (2) to produce a video that leaves them wanting more.

1. Since your highlight video is a compilation of plays, make sure you present your best plays first. From the time the video begins, you have about 15 seconds to get a coach's attention. If nothing sparks his interest right away, he'll turn your video off.

2. Make yourself easy to identify. Add a spot shadow and/or freeze the tape before each play and highlight yourself with an arrow. If coaches can't easily identify you, they will turn the tape off and move on to another player's video.

3. Trim excess video before and after each play.

4. Display your jersey number and complete contact information at the beginning and end of the video.

5. Keep the highlight tape under 4 minutes. If coaches like what they see in your short highlights, they may request a complete game tape. Make sure you have your best game film on file.

6. Make your video available online so that coaches can easily access it. Unless a coach requests a DVD, do not mail DVDs. Instead upload your highlight video to a video-hosting site, such as YouTube, and send the link to coaches. The easier you make the viewing process, the more you increase your chances of coaches watching it.

7. Include a soundtrack if you want. (Most college coaches will view on mute).

An Athlete Profile and Cover Letter *tell* coaches about you, but they want to *see* your talents for themselves. Since "action speaks louder than words," your highlight video can be the booming voice that communicates your athletic distinction the loudest.

BETWEEN THE LINES

You've probably heard the old adage, "read between the lines." When collegiate coaches view your highlight video, they "read between the lines" on your game film to assess your athletic qualities. When coaches "read between the lines" on your cover letter and athlete profile, they learn more about the individual overall qualities that set you apart from your competition.

For example, if your cover letter and profile contain typos, misspelled words, grammatical errors, or anything short of accuracy, then coaches receive a clear message: you lack attention to detail.

If you ramble in your cover letter instead of getting to the point and concisely stating your objective, then coaches receive a clear message: you lack focus.

If you opt to write a generic "Dear Coach" letter instead of personalizing each letter with the coach's name and team, then coaches receive a clear message: you're lazy.

Needless to say, coaches have zero interest in handing out NCAA scholarships to lazy, unfocused players who are not detail oriented. You wouldn't consider including clips on your highlight video of you dropping the ball. So don't let other aspects of your self-promotion display a lack of attention to detail either.

THE SOCIAL MEDIA RECRUITING MODEL

The tools for recruiting yourself have changed dramatically since I graduated high school in 2006. When I was marketing myself to college coaches, I completed the process the old fashioned way: printing 50 personalized cover letters and athlete profiles for my college choices, copying 50 DVD's, 50 packets, and by sending 50 packages by traditional mail. This process was time consuming and expensive.

Today you can accomplish the same tasks on your computer. You have access to the most powerful medium the world has ever known – Social Media – which has forever transformed the recruiting process for college football.

HOW TO MAKE SOCIAL MEDIA WORK FOR YOU

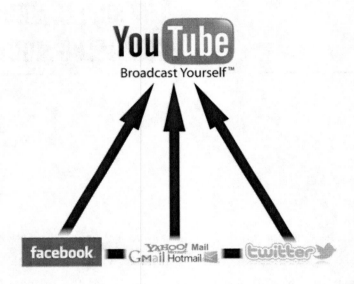

For coaches, social media is an efficient way to connect, recruit, and collect information about players. For you – the player – YouTube, Twitter, Facebook, (the big three) are revolutionary tools that give you the freedom to control and update your information as well as establish a personal rapport with coaches.

Your goal is to create a professional medium for informing coaches more about you and stimulating communication between you and coaches. Post regularly but use good judgment when posting anything online. A couple of good posting topics include announcing your recent academic or sports accomplishments and sending congratulatory messages about collegiate wins. But likewise be selective which high school friends have access to your recruitment pages. Make sure you monitor your pages regularly and promptly remove any posts or comments that may give coaches a negative impression of you. Depending on your privacy settings, coaches may still be able to view your personal social media pages. You can either change your privacy settings or delete any controversial posts, comments or pictures from your private pages. Let social media work for you and not against you.

With this in mind, I created the Social Media Recruiting Model. This model is based on using the "Big 3" — Facebook, Twitter, and YouTube — to create a free web-based platform that will allow you to connect with a wide coaching audience and effectively promote yourself.

Create your Facebook and Twitter pages as your online resume. Use these pages to post your highlight video and reach out to coaches – particularly those recruiting your area. The more you turn up the volume on quality visibility, the more coaches will notice. When you market yourself professionally and have the athletic/academic stats to back it up, your potential for getting recruited is greatly enhanced.

Protect the integrity of your social media pages, Otherwise you can sabotage your marketing efforts. Coaches are looking for extraordinary recruits – players who display exceptional talent on the field and a high level of moral character off the field. They're not looking for party rockers or players that could bring a lot of baggage to their college team. So make sure your posts on social media do not reflect negatively of you in any way.

Although problem players are nothing new in collegiate and professional football, social media now offers coaches the advantage of evaluating a player's value system while assessing his talent. This gives coaches a better edge for avoiding obvious problem players so they can focus on potential recruits that are more positively well rounded.

You are – in the coaches' eyes – what you post on Facebook, Twitter, and YouTube.

PAID RECRUITING SERVICES

Paid recruiting services are different from recruiting sites like Scout.com and Rivals.com. Recruiting services charge you a large fee to host your video content on their site. And they claim to have connections with college coaches who view their sites. Basically, subscription based online recruiting services will charge you a large monthly fee to do what this book teaches you how to accomplish on your own for free.

Some of you with extra money may wonder why you should put in the extra work of recruiting yourself if you can easily spend a few hundred dollars to hire a recruiting service to do it for you. The reason is simple. No matter how much money you pay, these services are not going to care about YOUR scholarship endeavors and outcome as much as you do. Also some college coaches consider these sites a poor reflection of the athlete's motivation and desire.

Coaches are looking for players who want work hard and earn their own way. YouTube, Facebook, and Twitter are all you need to successfully create a FREE web-based platform to market your skills to colleges and universities around the country.

WHAT BIG TIME COLLEGE FOOTBALL COACHES SAY ABOUT SOCIAL MEDIA & RECRUITING

The advantage of social media and recruiting is a two-way street. It doesn't just help you establish point and click contact with college coaches; it helps college coaches establish and maintain contact with you as well. And it gives them a broader view of each potential recruit. Here's what some of the nation's top collegiate coaches say about social media and the role its playing in their recruiting efforts:

Virginia's Mike London: "I'm on Facebook, Twitter, LinkedIn, and you name it. We're Skyping and doing all those things. If it's allowable by the NCAA, then you can use every social network means necessary to get your messages across. You will find out more about guys on Facebook and Twitter sometimes than you will having a 10-minute conversation with them because a lot of times they will let their guard down and show a side maybe you haven't thought about before. Social Media networks are now something that is very prevalent in recruiting."

Florida State's Jimbo Fisher: "I think it's huge in recruiting. It all is. Whether or not you like Social Media, it's here to stay. And it's something you have to deal with and learn to adapt to."

Ohio State's Urban Meyer: "Recruiting is about relationships and communications — and Social Media is a big part of it right now. I think it's huge. I don't do a big part of it myself, but my staff does a lot of it. We're very involved in all that stuff."

Texas A&M's Kevin Sumlin: "It's a pretty big deal. I've been on Twitter for a long time. For me, it's an ability to deliver a message, to get information out about our program not only to recruits but our fan base and alumni. The price is right, too. It's instantaneous. We utilize Twitter as more of an informational guide to update fans, prospects and our alumni base on videos, upcoming events and news items. I think Facebook is more of a communicative tool than Twitter [with recruits]."

Vanderbilt's James Franklin: "The society we live in now, how kids are growing up, Social Media is a huge part of their lives. It's a huge part of what they do and how they communicate. So we embrace it. It's a part of what we're going to do here. It's another way to sell your product and see what you have to offer. It's another way to build relationships and get to know people. You can learn a lot about kids by going onto their Facebook accounts and following them on Twitter. It's just another source of information."

North Carolina's Larry Fedora: "I think it's huge now in recruiting, I really do. If you're not using it, then you're falling behind every day because it's a way to stay in contact with kids. Both of those, Facebook and Twitter, go to their phones so you're able to communicate with them legally. If you're not doing that in recruiting, you're way behind the curve."

Missouri's Gary Pinkel: "I think it's become pretty big, as far as communication [with prospects]. There are certain things you're allowed to do within the rules. You're not allowed to text but you can certainly Facebook, email, Twitter and things like that. Those things are legal. From a communications standpoint, it's big. Not just from the standpoint of the University of

Missouri but for anybody. It certainly gives coaches and student-athletes more opportunities to talk to one another."

Quotes taken from:
http://blogs.ajc.com/recruiting/2012/05/21/how-big-of-a-role-does-social-media-play-in-football-recruiting/

ESTABLISH THE FOUNDATION OF YOUR SELF-MARKETING EFFORTS

UNDERSTAND YOUR PERSONAL BRAND

A corporate brand is not just a name. It's an identity. For example, when you hear the name Chevrolet, you automatically think things about the vehicle. Some of them are positive, while some may be negative. You may mentally see an Impala, or you may visualize a Suburban, or you may have a thought of a Corvette. The brand is more than a name for a division of General Motors. It also defines the character of the vehicle in the minds of people who hear it.

Likewise, your personal brand is not a logo. It's what defines you as a student athlete. Your personal brand includes – but is not limited to – the position(s) you play as well as your individual talent, strengths, weaknesses, grades, character, and extracurricular activities. In short, your brand is a mental snapshot of the athletic and academic value you offer college coaches. Like any product on the market – whether it's athletic shoes or vehicles – value added branding will give you the competitive edge.

CHOOSE A PROFILE PICTURE THAT SPEAKS FOR YOU

Your social media profile picture needs to make a strong visual statement.

You may tend to periodically change your profile picture on your personal social media pages. But the object of your college recruiting pages is to paint a picture of yourself in the minds of coaches. Since repetition strengthens branding, pick an impactful profile picture and post it on Facebook, Twitter, and YouTube. In order to maximize your branding efforts, post an action shot of you playing in a game that clearly shows your jersey number. This will not only draw attention to your picture; it will help coaches easily identify you when watching game film.

SELLING YOUR BRAND ON THE "BIG 3"

Aside from texting and email correspondence – Facebook, Twitter, and YouTube are three preferred mediums that offer ideal formats for effectively building your personal brand.

YOUTUBE

YouTube has changed the face of recruiting by providing the medium for coaches to see you in action in order to evaluate your skill set and determine if you're a good fit for their program. In most recruiting scenarios, coaches will want to see

you play live. Providing them with great video will help you get
to that point.

HOW TO UPLOAD YOUR VIDEO TO YOUTUBE

- Go to www.youtube.com and create an account.
  For your account name, use something you won't be
  embarrassed for a coach to see. Your real name will
  work fine. Then select the upload option.

- Select a video from either your hard drive or from your
  disk drive.

- Appropriately title the video: Your Name; Class; Sport;
  Position.

- Write a brief description of your video. You can include
  your sport, position, several important stats, height,
  weight and your class.

- Suitably tag the video "Recruiting Video" and "(your
  sport) Highlights."

- Select the category: Sports.

- Set the privacy settings to public.

- Leave the "Licensing and Rights Ownership" set to
  "Standard YouTube License."

You will receive a link to the location of your video. Now
you are ready to share your video with coaches via Facebook,
Twitter, and email.

After coaches view a highlight film, their next step is to view your full game film. You can upload your full game film to YouTube. But you will need to break it up in three or four parts due to YouTube time limits on videos. This does require some skill with video editing. But it's an extremely efficient way to distribute your game film to coaches. Don't be intimidated by the editing process. There is an easy-to-use, free video editor on YouTube.

Make sure to include your contact information on your YouTube Channel. Coaches will likely find your channel because you contacted them and provided a link. For the benefit of any coaches that may be arbitrarily browsing YouTube, they need to know how to reach you if they're interested. By always covering the contact bases, you maximize your recruitment chances.

FACEBOOK

Facebook is the premier social networking site for connecting you to your target coaches and teams. Once you have your football-recruiting page up and in peak working order – the next step is to direct traffic from your target market to your page. Now that you're in the business of selling yourself to a college football team, networking is the name of the game.

BASIC CONCEPT

The concept of networking is a vital sales tool. The business philosophy is "it's not WHAT you know; it's WHO you know." Forward thinking marketers have historically taken the opportunity to reach out to prospective buyers by attending events that offered large captive audiences. While nothing will ever replace human interaction, Facebook adds a new dimension to networking.

Most college teams now have a Facebook page that contains photos from competitions and regular updates. By "liking" each team that's on your target-marketing list, you begin putting yourself in a prime position to network, market yourself, and gain recognition. Not only will your involvement in these pages broaden your view of each college's program, it will give you the opportunity to get your name out there by "liking" certain posts and possibly "friending" current team members. You never know who can help you get your foot in a coach's door.

SEARCH AND CONNECT WITH COACHES

Unless you're already a highly recruited athlete, coaches aren't going to go out of their way to friend you on Facebook and follow you on Twitter. You must take the initiative and make the first move.

Before you friend or follow every coach you can randomly find, keep in mind that successful networking is all about quality and not necessarily quantity. Therefore begin by creating a priority list of the top 50 colleges you'd like to attend most. This list should contain schools that are realistically a good fit with your individual talents and capabilities. For example, if you are a quality D2 athlete, focus more on D2 teams than D1 powerhouses such as Alabama, LSU, USC, Ohio State, Texas, or Alabama.

After you've compiled your Top 50, go to each team's website and list names of the head coach, recruiting coordinator, and position(s) coach under each school. While friending and following head coaches is recommended, you should likewise friend and follow each college's recruiting coordinator and applicable position coach on your Top 50 because they are the ones who will generally review your Athlete profile and Highlight Video first.

LIKE, SHARE AND COMMENT ON COACH'S LINKS AND UPDATES

When a coach or connection posts a link or status update on his page, you have the option to respond, which gets your name in front of that person. For example, if you push the Share button, the link appears on your page as well. If you push the Like button, your name is listed among others who liked the link or comment. Or you can post comments on status updates.

The more you tactfully do any of these, the more visible you'll become to these coaches and people in their networks. And let's face it, visibility is the foundation for recruiting yourself. But there's a fine line between tactfully responding and insincerely sucking up. And coaches can instantly tell the difference. If you Like, Share, or Comment on every post, you'll gain the wrong kind of visibility. Respond accurately and intelligently.

TWITTER

First and foremost, I highly recommend you Google, "50 Twitter Tips for Division I Student-Athletes" by Tom Satkowiak. Most of his tips are applicable to high school athletes. Take 10 minutes to read it before you setup a Twitter account for recruiting purposes.

BASIC CONCEPT

Twitter is a great tool that provides players with a quick and easy way to share thoughts and follow college coaches via tweets. Begin marketing yourself on Twitter by creating an account that's separate from your personal Twitter account and use it for recruiting purposes only. Coaches can keep close track of what you have to say by following you, and similarly you can decide which coaches you wish to follow. Twitter can offer you a deeper sense of each athletic program because coaches and programs generally update their Twitter account more often and share more personal thoughts. Just like Facebook, the key is to interact and show interest. Mention coaches and programs in your tweets, re-tweet their good results, and show that you are serious about being a part of their team.

YOUR PROFILE MATTERS

The quality of your Twitter profile is critical because college coaches typically check out your profile before they decide to follow you. Aside from a game-shot profile picture that visibly displays your jersey number, you need to write a brief but well-crafted bio, which will appear next to your name. For example, "#58 Class of _____. All-District Defensive-End. 6'2" 250lbs. Bartlesville, OK. YouTube Highlight Video"

FOLLOW COACHES FIRST

You'll need to take the lead by searching and following the same head coaches, recruiting coordinators, and position(s) coaches that you friended on Facebook from the Top 50 college teams on your target marketing list. They'll receive a

Twitter alert that you're following them, which may prompt them to check out your Athlete profile and YouTube channel.

FOLLOW SPORTS WRITERS

Aside from searching for your Top 50 college coaches on Facebook and Twitter, friend and follow writers of big time recruiting sites like Rivals.com and Scout.com. Since these writers actively look for top recruits that haven't been scouted in high school, they can be instrumental in helping college coaches notice you.

YOU ARE WHAT YOU TWEET

Twitter followers will judge you by your tweets. Since coaches are in the business of winning football games and keeping their jobs, their goal is to recruit players who are winners on and off the field. So keep your tweets/posts positive. Make sure the content reflects your work ethic, integrity and maturity. Instead of trash talking or responding to trolls – which turns coaches away – use your Twitter exposure to report your own recruiting news.

For example, you could tweet about an upcoming college visit, scholarship offers, a productive practice, a good grade on a test, stats of your last game, or the time and location of next week's game. The list of positive tweeting/posting options are endless. The benefits of productive tweeting are equally as endless. You're keeping coaches updated on your accomplishments. You're appearing regularly on coaches' news feeds. And you're thereby maximizing Twitter features to promote yourself. The more positive your tweets, the more coaches may want to see that positive attitude and production in person.

SEND LINKS

The main purpose for marketing yourself to college football coaches on Twitter is to lead them to your YouTube channel where they can learn more about you and view your highlight video. The best way to accomplish this is by sending a link of your YouTube channel directly to a coach through Facebook, Twitter, Email, and text messages.

MAKE SOCIAL MEDIA WORK FOR YOU

Channel your inner promoter by taking advantage of every interactive feature social networking offers. After you friend or follow coaches, let them know you're reading their posts by posting your comments, hitting the "Like" button on Facebook, re-tweeting some of their posts or sending direct messages. This doesn't just show coaches that you're interested in becoming part of their team. It shows coaches that you're highly interested.

EMAIL

Take the same precautions here as you did with your Twitter handle by making sure that your email address is appropriate. While this may seem like a small thing, it could make the difference between a coach opening your email or deleting it unread. Your email address name is often the first impression a coach will get about you. A first impression is a lasting impression. And a negative first impression is one of the hardest things to overcome in the recruiting process. So make sure your email address reflects maturity and professionalism. You can't go wrong by simply using your first and last name because that's the best and easiest way for a coach to identify you at first glance.

Furthermore the body of your emails must contain proper grammar and correct punctuation. The cover letter that you previously crafted will probably be the first email you send a coach. But all of your messages must clearly explain why you are contacting the coach. Refrain from using texting short-cuts – like "U" for you. Instead spell out every word. Before a coach considers awarding you a college scholarship, he wants to know that you are educated enough to write an email and that you are capable of representing his program to the highest degree.

Email coaches every week, even if they do not reply to your emails. Persistence is key. Start by picking a manageable number of new coaches to email each week – like three to five or more if you think you can handle it. But don't overload yourself. Like most student athletes, you're probably busy with studying, sports, other extracurricular activities and a social life. But recruiting yourself demands even more time, so budget your time wisely and set adequate time aside for recruiting. Playing college sports is even more time consuming. Budgeting your time now – while you're in high school – is one more way of preparing yourself for college.

Whenever you email a coach, always attach your Athlete profile, include a link to your online Highlight Video and include your name//graduating class/position(s) in the subject line.

EMAIL SUBJECT

Your email subject line can determine whether or not a coach will open your email. So put your most strategic foot forward and devise short, concise subject lines that will appeal to college coaches. Include your name, graduating class, and position(s) in the email subject. Avoid email subject lines such as "I'm the best, Coach" or "Check me out, Coach!" Keep your subject lines as professional as possible.

Aside from continually adding new coaches to your email list, use your recruiting time to follow up with coaches you have already emailed. If a coach responds to you, reply as soon as possible.

For branding and consistency, carefully craft your email signature and include it at the bottom of every recruitment email you send. For example:

Your Name
Phone Number
Email Address
High School Name and Address
YouTube Link

WHEN TO START THE RECRUITING PROCESS

My web-based social media model requires that you accomplish three steps before beginning the marketing process on YouTube, Facebook, and Twitter. You will need:

1. A productive season on varsity

2. An Athlete Profile that details athletic and academic achievements

3. A quality Highlight Video with game film ready for coaches' requests

Once you meet those criteria, the beginning of your junior year is the ideal time to begin the recruiting process because that's when coaches begin looking at athletic statistics and college admission departments start assessing academic achievements. If you wait until your senior year, you can have a few more challenges – particularly with many large D1 schools that may have already awarded most of their scholarships. While an athlete's junior year is preferred, it's not a do or die situation. But you'll be under much more pressure to excel during your senior season. You still have plenty of opportunities to turn heads and earn a football scholarship, even from D1 schools.

How to jump-start your recruitment NOW: meet with your high school counselor and develop an academic game plan that satisfies all the requirements of the NCAA. You must complete three academic goals to be eligible for an athletic scholarship:

1. You must pass your high school graduation requirements.

2. Your GPA and SAT/ACT scores must meet eligibility requirements. Some colleges and universities have different requirements.

3. NCAA Eligibility Center standards must be met. These are available at the NCAA Clearing House website: www.ncaaclearinghouse.com.

This point is critical and I cannot stress it strongly enough: the longer you wait to send your information to college coaches, the smaller your chance of getting an athletic scholarship. As a high school player, your first goal is to make sure college coaches are aware of you. While sending your information early does not guarantee a scholarship, it does increase your odds of getting on the school's recruiting database. After you are in the system, you'll have a much better chance of being further evaluated by coaches.

HOW DO COACHES DECIDE WHOM TO RECRUIT?

College coaches want to recruit those who have proven themselves on the field and in the classroom. Coaches recruit prospects that fit their coaching philosophy, system, and style of play. They put recruits through an evaluation process that examines everything – height, weight, speed, position(s), academics, and game statistics.

When college coaches receive your cover letter, athlete resume, and highlight video, they assess your materials in the same way employers evaluate resumes submitted by prospective employees. After weighing your athletic and academic strengths, coaches determine whether or not your talents can fill their team's specific needs. Some of the factors coaches take into consideration are the number of graduating seniors on the roster, the number and quality of athletes on their team, athletes playing your position and the amount of financial aid that is available. Like employers, coaches recruit players that can fill needed positions. Though you may not be a good fit for some teams, you could be a great fit for others.

College coaches begin the recruiting season in January with about 1,500 prospects. Throughout the months, they add and delete potential recruits until they chisel their list down to the exact number of new players they need.

Coaches use a variety of avenues to find recruits. They might begin with names of All-District, All-Region, and All-State players statewide or in surrounding states. Coaches might research lists of names that their scouts have identified as possible recruits. They also rely on observation from their own camps, which are on-campus events run by their coaching staff - (discussed in a later chapter). And coaches especially depend on information, such as a highlight video, game film, and athlete resume submitted directly from high school student-athletes.

When a college coach is interested in you, he'll ask you to complete an athlete questionnaire – either online or on a paper form – that will tell him more about you and allows him to access your academic transcripts. While receiving questionnaires from college football programs is an exciting first step, it doesn't mean you are being recruited. It just means you are on the school's mailing list and you are being evaluated. Coaches extend the same questionnaire request to hundreds, sometimes thousands, of potential recruits.

Thoroughly complete all athlete questionnaires and return them as soon as possible. When the football office receives the completed questionnaire, your name and information will be added into their recruiting database for future reference. Coaches measure your interest in their program by how quickly you respond to any contact initiated by them. The same applies to any additional documents requested by the admissions office, financial aid office, or the NCAA. When college coaches must decide between student-athletes who are athletically and academically comparable, they usually choose those who have demonstrated discipline and maturity in their communications with the coach.

QUESTIONNAIRES

Completing recruitment questionnaires is one of the simplest ways to get on a coach's radar and confirm your interest in his program. This also puts the team on your radar because – after you submit your questionnaire – you'll begin receiving information on upcoming events, camps or games that the college hosts. By participating in some of these college events, you can boost your exposure and increase your chances of meeting college coaches. You can voluntarily complete and submit questionnaires online by visiting the official website of each college's football program. Don't expect a response from a coach just because you filled out a questionnaire. Follow up through Facebook, Twitter, and email.

SCHOLARSHIPS BREED SCHOLARSHIPS

Getting your first football scholarship offer – regardless of the school's size – is a huge step toward gaining more scholarship recognition from other schools. Even if a Division II school offers you your first football scholarship, coaches from larger Division I schools will soon start evaluating you more closely because another college coach has recognized and validated you as a valuable addition to his team. When you've been offered your first football scholarship, make sure every other school that's on your Top 50 knows about it through Facebook and Twitter. Contact athlete recruiting websites like Scout.com and Rivals.com and let them know you've been offered because they'll spread the news by posting it on their sites, informing other colleges and vastly increasing your market value. Coaches don't want to miss out on recruiting skilled players.

RECRUITING SERVICES

The two primary types of recruiting services include online companies that charge high school student-athletes a fee in exchange for providing player information to college football programs and subscription services – such as Rivals.com and Scout.com – that offer online news about recruits and message boards for fans. Writers from Rivals and Scout can be extremely beneficial to enhancing social media exposure. Here are a few important writers from Rivals.com and Scout.com you should follow on Twitter and friend on Facebook: Dallas Jackson (@ RivalsDallas), Mike Farrell, Bob Litchenfels, Matt Alkire, and Jeremy Crabtree. When you gain any exposure on these websites – no matter how small – coaches perceive it as valuable information they can look at before beginning recruitment preparation.

PHONE CONVERSATION & VOICEMAIL

The benefits of calling coaches are mutual. For coaches, your calls enable them to put a personality to your name, jersey number and Highlight Video. For you, the calls take your relationship with coaches to a higher level. Since some recruits are hesitant to call coaches, you can set yourself apart from them and gain a recruitment advantage by taking the initiative to make the call. Although talking on the phone with college coaches may seem awkward at first, you should begin to feel more comfortable after a few phone calls.

Ask specific questions. For example, if the team just played in a bowl game, ask the coach about the experience and how it helped his team. Information you learn about coaches and teams on Facebook and Twitter will help you expand talking points in your phone conversations. Talking to a coach should be a two-way street that gives you both a better sense of one another. Yet you need to remember that you aren't talking to your best friend. You're talking to a professional contact. So exercise good judgment, maturity and formal protocol. Don't keep coaches on the phone too long. And avoid lapses of silence on your end. If the coach seems distracted, tell him that you'll call back another time – when he isn't so busy. He'll appreciate your perception and thoughtfulness.Despite your calls to coaches, be prepared for the day a coach will call you. Keep a prepared list of answers handy to questions that coaches may ask you as well as questions that you want to ask the coach about the school or the program.

Here is a sampling of questions that you may consider asking:

1. What is the depth chart like at my position?

2. What is the coach's philosophy?

3. What position am I on the recruiting depth chart?

4. What is the university known for academically?

5. Are tutors available for athletes?

6. What's the average fan attendance during home games?

Think about questions a coach may possibly ask you. For example:

1. Do you plan to re-take the ACT/SAT?

2. What is your coach's cell phone number?

3. Tell me about your recent injuries.

4. Are you willing to change positions in college?

5. Are you willing to walk on?

6. If you're offered a partial scholarship, will you commit to the program?

Rehearse your response to these questions. And answer each question completely and clearly. You want to come across as intelligent, articulate, and interested in what the coach says. In order to better prepare for a coach's call, try contacting current college athletes to get an idea about what questions to expect.

In the event that a coach reaches your voicemail when he calls, make sure that a professionally delivered voicemail script greets him. Your script doesn't have to be elaborate. It can simply say, "This is _____. Sorry I missed your call. Please leave your name and number and I will get back to you as soon as possible." Just make sure that you record the message instead of using the factory voicemail setting on your phone or answering machine. This shows coaches that you are mature and professional even if they get your voicemail.

FOLLOW UP

You need to follow up with coaches regularly in order to keep your name fresh in their minds. Coaches contact numerous recruits in a short amount of time. If you fail to properly follow up with a coach, you could fall off his radar.

Follow up emails are equally as important. This template can be used as a guide for writing follow-up emails to the college or university coaches that contact you:

Date:
Coach's Name/College/University Name/Address
Dear Coach _____,

I was excited to hear from you. I am writing this letter to tell you of my continued interest in playing (name the sport) for _____College/University.

Attached is this season's schedule. Here is my coach's telephone number and email address _____. He/she is available to answer any questions you may have.

(Include updates, highlights, new achievements or awards, invitations, improved grades, etc.).

I look forward to continued discussions regarding how I can contribute to your team.

Thank you for taking the time to read this letter and for considering me.

Sincerely,
Your Name
Phone Number
Email Address
High School Name and Address
YouTube Link

FOOTBALL CAMPS

During the summer months, college football programs offer on-campus camps for high school and lower division athletes. Camps enable college coaches to evaluate speed, power, courage, and strength of prospects. Showcasing your skills in front of coaches is a great opportunity to gain immediate recognition as a potential scholarship athlete. Summer camps are one of few times during the year when college coaches can freely interact with prospective athletes who are on their campuses. Summer football camps have been referred to as "meat markets" because players are weighed, measured, and herded around from drill to drill like a stockyard of cattle ready to be auctioned off. College coaches want to make sure they're making the best investment before signing a recruit, so you must prepare yourself physically and mentally for a very challenging environment. Schedules and dates for football camps are usually listed on the university's website. If you can't find these dates, email coaches and request this information.

MAKE SURE YOU KNOW WHAT KIND OF CAMP YOU'RE ATTENDING

College Camps are held by college coaches and provide athletes an opportunity to play in front of the coaches they want to get recruited by. This is the type of camp that most high school athletes are looking for because it puts them directly in front of scouts. If you happen to attend one of these camps, prepare yourself. Eat right; get plenty of sleep; and prepare to work harder on the field than you ever have before. There is no such thing as over preparation when showcasing your skills.

Showcase Tournaments – or Combines – are held by a third party such as Nike or Adidas. These camps draw more scouts from a wide array of colleges. But getting noticed is a challenge. You will definitely need to proactively introduce yourself to college coaches. Less popular combines than those presented by major sport merchandisers charge a significant amount of money and do very little for your recruiting efforts. Even though these camps may sound worthless, they are not. They may do little for your recruiting effort, but they provide experience in meeting coaches and showcasing your talents during a camp.

CHOOSE CAMPS WISELY

Not all college football camps are created equal, so make sure you choose the ones that will maximize your visibility and recruiting potential. As a sophomore or junior in high school, your primary objective should be gaining exposure in front of college coaches.

Mini-camps are the best way to accomplish this. Mini-camps are designed to last only a day or less. They provide a great opportunity for players to prove themselves, showcase their talent to college coaches, and get recruited.

Multi-day camps – which usually run for three days – emphasize basic fundamentals and technique. Attending mini-camps, opposed to multi-day camps, are much more beneficial for your scholarship efforts and save you a lot of time and money. I decided which mini-camps to attend by searching for information on the official websites of college football programs. Mini-camps camps are affordable with fees running from $30 to $50, which is a small investment for chasing your dream of receiving an athletic scholarship.

With exception to Special Teams Camps, you will benefit most by registering for mini-camps that are sponsored directly by NCAA schools. Avoid **exposure camps** that are produced by businesses claiming to increase your recruitment opportunities by distributing your name and stats to colleges and universities. These camps often try to lure you from one camp to another by basically saying, "You qualified for our next camp." They're in it for your money and coaches have little regards for the stats they receive from these companies. **Special Teams Camps** deserve your consideration though. Coaches love players who can add several dimensions to their program, especially those who can play quality Special Teams.

Make sure you get the best results possible by researching which tests and drills are going to be run at a mini-camp. Then practice those events before the day of the camp. A poor performance or lack of preparation could cost you a scholarship. Players are typically measured for height/weight and put through basic tests – like the 40-yard dash, vertical jump, pro shuttle, and the number of times they can bench press either 185 or 225 pounds.

After you've determined what camps you want to attend, start making connections with the coaching staff – if you haven't already. In case you've previously spoken to coaches who have shown interest, you may be wise to go to their camps first. When you walk into a camp, you want the coach to already know who you are and be familiar with your skills. Coaches will be ten times more likely to watch and scout you at a camp after they already know who you are and watched your video on YouTube.

WARNING ...

College football coaches invite many players to their camps, which is one reason I highly recommend communicating with coaches before attending. At camps, coaches mostly scout athletes with whom they already have an open line of communication. If a coach hasn't seen your video and previously had multiple conversations with you, they're less likely to recruit you.

This is one of many instances where connecting with coaches via social media, email, text, and phone calls will pay off. When deciding which camps you want to attend, you must honestly gauge your level of play. Don't sell yourself short, but if you are not a NCAA Division 1 level player do not attend NCAA Division 1 camps because that will be a waste of time and somewhat embarrassing. Instead stick with camps in your own league so you have the best opportunity to realistically earn a scholarship. You must also consider camps sponsored by schools you are truly interested in attending and the coaches in which you have already built a rapport.

Coaches recruit many players each year. But they may be looking to fill only one or two critical positions on their team's roster. It's your job to research the program and measure your chances of playing if you are recruited. Look at the seniors and juniors that are set to graduate when you will be entering college. Determine how many of them play your position. If you see a college roster that is full of freshman and sophomore athletes that play your position, you may want to look for opportunities at another college.

After you have had some communication with a coach, ask him how many other athletes he's recruiting at your position. One of the first things a coach will ask you is what other schools are recruiting you. Make this a two-way street by communicating with a coach and finding out where you stand on their recruiting board. After you find out where you stand, you can decide if you want to invest more time in that program or if you want to move on to another school.

HOW TO STAND OUT AT CAMP

Standing out from the competition during camp is crucial for gaining recognition from college coaches as a potential scholarship recruit. A lot of high school players become intimidated when they're given a chance to perform in front of college coaches. This will not earn you a football scholarship. You must hustle and go all out if you want to grab the coaches' attention. Sprint between drills. Be the first in line. Always finish the drills at full speed. Be respectful. And listen when a coach is talking. The goal of camp is to gain recognition from the coaches as a scholarship athlete. You only have one chance. Get as many reps as you can.

I stood out from other players at camp by performing more reps than anyone else during drills. I always tried to be the first in line. And after I completed a drill – instead of going to the back of the line – I'd go to the third or fourth person in front and say, "Hey, coach wants me to go again." By the end of camp, I had completed about three times as many drills as anyone else, which meant I had about three times as much exposure to coaches than anyone else. You can do this too. Don't worry what other recruits at these camps think. Do everything you can to get more reps and quality exposure.

WHAT TO EXPECT AT CAMP

Try to arrive at camp about an hour early so you can stretch and prepare yourself mentally. After you sign in, you'll be weighed and measured. Coaches usually begin the combines by dividing athletes into groups according to position and physical size.

The first part of combine testing normally involves about six different tests, which include: vertical jump, 40-yard dash, pro shuttle, broad jump, and bench press reps with 185 lbs or 225 lbs.

After combine testing, the coaches generally provide one-on-one coaching to players according to their positions while also evaluating their effort, athletic ability, and comprehension skills. This is a great opportunity to learn from coaches, so be sure to ask questions and listen intently when spoken to. Be respectful: always say "Yes sir," and "Thank you, sir."

Later, quarterbacks, receivers, running backs, linebackers, and defensive backs compete in 7-on-7 drills while the offensive and defensive linemen compete against each other in one-on-one pass rushing and blocking drills.

One-day camps usually last 5-6 hours and typically end after the 7-on-7 drills and one-on-one pass rushing/blocking drills. Your goal for the single day combines isn't necessarily to leave with a scholarship offer, but to establish yourself as a player coaches recognize as a potential scholarship recruit. Stand out and make an impression by taking mental notes and using them as talking points when communicating with coaches on the phone, through email, or Twitter and Facebook messages.

During camp, you may notice some of the college coaches talking one-on-one with other players. You may think these players are receiving special attention while you're being ignored. I thought this too until I realized what the coaches are really doing. It's called the "eyeball test" – when a coach sizes up a player in person.

TIPS FOR COMBINE TESTING

During camp, you're competing against hundreds of players who want the same thing you want – a football scholarship. Here are a few ways that you can get an edge over your competition:

1. Show up to camp conditioned and in shape. Make it a habit to eat healthy, sleep well and maximize your reps in practice and the weight room.

2. Wear the lightest cleats possible (preferably receiver cleats) while running the 40-yard dash. They usually shave off at least .10 seconds.

3. Run the 40 in compression shorts to minimize wind resistance. (You've seen the NFL combines.)

4. Get your last name printed on the back of your shirt. Coaches can easily put a name to a face if they see it often.

5. Wrap your wrists before maxing on the bench press. The wraps allow the stabilizing muscles in your forearm to rest, which will give you a few extra reps.

6. Be fluid in your movements. Coaches hate when players run rigid. Be flexible, stay low, and run smooth.

7. Show respect and be a coachable player. Don't make excuses. Look the coach in the eyes, take mental notes, and reply with, "Yes sir."

8. Compete. The best way to make a lasting impression by the end of camp is to maximize the amount of effort you put out. This is your championship game.

9. Finish each drill at full speed. Go a second or two past the whistle to ensure you are through, while maximizing each rep.

10. After camp, ask your position coach what he thinks you need to work on. Use this feedback to improve weak points in your performance.

PERFORMANCE COMBINES

Performance combines are scheduled events, at which high school players are timed and measured in a variety of physical tests. Some are offered at no cost while others charge a large sum of money. The Nike combine is a scheduled event in which the country's top high school football players have their athleticism evaluated through physical testing and given a "SPARQ" rating. SPARQ is an acronym for speed, power, agility, reaction, and quickness.

Nike's invitation only combines are held in the spring exclusively for high school juniors. The NCAA doesn't allow college coaches to attend these events. But scouting services and media – such as Scouts.com and Rivals.com – relate the results to college coaches. The camp consists of two parts: basic agility drills that focus on movements and skills related to each player's position and one-on-one drills for offensive and defensive lineman, as well as 7-on-7 drills for quarterbacks, receivers, linebackers and safeties. Getting invited to attend the Nike combine may be a difficult task. But attending the combine is great experience and media exposure.

Combines for high school players, like the Nike Camp, are extremely popular with the media but are not as meaningful to college coaches as you might expect. College coaches need more than a combine evaluation to properly assess a high school player. After all, players who participate in Nike Camps aren't wearing football pads and helmets. Your real evaluation comes from playing on the field with pads of course.

FACE-TO-FACE WITH THE COACH

If you've hustled on the field as a player, studied hard in the classroom as a student, and followed the steps outlined in *Recruit Yourself* to this point, you can expect to go to the next step. You can expect to be closer to meeting a college football coach, the man holding your potential scholarship, face-to-face.

UNOFFICIAL VISITS

College football coaches invite hundreds of potential recruits to unofficial visits each year, which is a visit you take to a college campus at your own expense. Visits can be taken anytime and as many times as you want. They offer great opportunities to check out the school and get a chance to meet some of the coaches. While you're on an unofficial visit, the athletic department can give you up to three tickets to a sporting event but no other perks or gifts.

Here's a small tip that helped me when I was being recruited. Whenever a college or university invited me for an unofficial visit, I'd go to that school's website and print off the coaches' picture roster. I'd memorize their last names and faces so that when I arrived I always made a great first impression by being the first to address them by their last names (Coach _____) and then introduce myself.

During your visit, network with players and coaches by friending them on Facebook and following them Twitter. Tweet and post a couple of statuses about how well your official visit is going. Be sure you're connected with other college coaches you want to be recruited by and they'll see this and recognize other schools are recruiting you. Also dress appropriately. Present yourself in a way that will give coaches confidence in your character.

OFFICIAL VISITS

Official visits are given to the players that coaches are seriously considering for scholarships. The NCAA allows one official visit per school and five total official visits that can only be taken during the athlete's senior year. During an official visit, the college can cover your trip expenses. Transportation includes paid airfare or reimbursing you for driving expenses. The college will pay for your hotel. And coaches will take you out to eat.

When you arrive for your official visit, a coach will greet you and take you to your hotel. During the day, assistant coaches will take you on a tour of the campus and show you around the facilities. Be sure to check out all the facilities that you'll use daily while on campus: classrooms, dorms, library, athletic facilities, dining facilities, and student union. This is not only when coaches get to know you as a person; it is when you get to know the college you'll possibly attend.

Later that night, you'll go out for dinner, talk with coaches and meet current players on the team. After dinner, you'll leave with one of the players who will introduce you to other players on the team. This is a great chance to ask their opinions of the coaches, practices, school, or location. Take the time to see what athletes do during their time off and get to know your potential teammates better. Network with players and coaches by friending them on Facebook and following them on Twitter. Tweet and post a couple of statuses about how well your official visit is going. If you're connected with other college coaches they'll see this and recognize other schools are recruiting you. This will make them want to recruit you too.

When you return home, I recommend writing the coaching staff a thank you note, whether you're offered a scholarship by that college or not. You can email your thank you note. But nothing sends a sincere message better than a hand written thank you note. College football teams invest a significant amount of money in official visits. Show your appreciation for the time and generosity that went into your visit.

MAINTAINING GOOD RELATIONSHIPS

Maintaining a good working relationship with your high school coaches is vital. This isn't a matter of being a mercenary or just about earning a college scholarship. It's a matter of good sportsmanship. When a college coach calls your high school coach, you do not want your current coach to say "That guy's unmotivated and selfish." You want him to say, "He really hustles on the field, and he's coachable. You'd be smart to get him on your team."

How do you do that? Start by being an accountable student-athlete. Do what your coach tells you to do. If you disagree with him, and you most certainly will at some point, discuss your disagreement with him calmly and politely. Attack problems, not people. If you don't understand something, ask questions. Schedule appointments to talk with your coach and teachers and ask them what you're doing right and what you're doing wrong. Relate their advice to your performance on and off the field. No one knows you better as a student-athlete than your high school coaches and teachers.

Be a team player. Remember, players don't win games, teams do. If you put yourself on the line for the team, it will reflect in your personal stats, and in your coach's mind. Always finish plays, regardless of what's happening on the field. For example, if you're a receiver and your quarterback calls a running play, block your opponent and don't stop until you hear a whistle regardless of what is happening behind you.

If anyone asks you about your opinion of your coach, say something positive. Whatever you say may get back to your coach. If your high school coach hears that you spoke negatively about him, it may filter up to a college coach. If you speak negatively about your high school coach, it may damage your standing as a scholarship recruit. If another player bad-mouths your coach, it's your opportunity to back your coach and show leadership.

If you maintain a good relationship with your high school coach and you work hard in every aspect on and off the field, he will recommend you to a college coach.

SELF-ASSESSMENT

It's true that not every high school football player will earn an athletic scholarship. It's also true that even some of the most talented players won't either. I remember a quote that was painted on the wall in my high school locker room that read, "Hard work beats talent when talent doesn't work hard." It's not unusual for an underdog player who lacks natural ability but has great discipline, toughness, grades, and performance to earn a scholarship over a highly talented athlete who lacks the underdog's qualities.

Throughout your life people will advise you to be realistic, take the safe route or give up trying. It's better to try a thousand times and fail than to have never tried at all. Who cares if there's a great chance of failure. If it's important to you, then it's worth going for. If you fail, at least you won't have any regrets because you'll know that you did everything you could to achieve your dreams.

Anyone can lure a coach to their YouTube channel and get their videos evaluated. The question is – will the coach take an interest in recruiting you after seeing your performance on the field? It's a good idea to assess your athletic potential for participating in collegiate athletics. At which level of competition could you expect to play? Where would you feel most comfortable? This will allow you to make more informed choices on which football programs to market yourself. You must honestly assess your athletic ability and realize the bottom line ultimately comes down to ON FIELD PRODUCTIVITY. As an individual you have to perform consistently at a high level during games in order to have any marketable value. Don't pursue D1 schools if you are not a D1 quality player. No matter what level university you play for, you will be making your dreams come true and getting an outstanding education on a scholarship.

WALKING ON

Most NCAA football programs allow walk-ons. If you are not offered a scholarship by the college of your choice, you can ask to join the team as a preferred walk-on, which is a preferred player that is enrolling at the college to play on the football team but does not have a scholarship offer. Walk-ons pay tuition for college like a non-athlete student unless the head coach awards them an athletic scholarship.

Before enrolling, check to see if the head coach is known for giving scholarships to deserving walk-ons. NCAA rules require walk-ons to have a passing GPA before the head coach can award them a football scholarship. Otherwise, the head coach decides if or when he awards a football scholarship to a walk-on that's based on work ethic and productivity on and off the field.

Throughout my college experience, I've seen guys walk on the football team and work harder than most scholarship players. They never skipped 6 AM practices. They attended grueling workouts. They went to every team meeting. And they maintain a high GPA throughout college while not even on scholarship like the rest of us. These are the caliber of walk-on players that college coaches award scholarships to.

JIM WENDLER: THE WALK ON

We will end this book with an inspiring story of a walk-on football player. This story will set the tone of the hard work you need to possess in your commitment to recruiting yourself in order of gaining a scholarship. The following is a true story from former University of Arizona football player Jim Wendler and his firsthand account of what life as a walk-on at a major university is all about. If you worked hard and put your full effort into gaining a scholarship and came up short, then becoming a walk-on may be your only shot at playing college ball. If so, you need to be prepared and Jim Wendler's story is one that will not only show you the hardships, but inspire you to put your full effort into anything you do in life. Here is his story:

* The following story is written by and courtesy of Jim Wendler on 4/23/2012 for the website "T-Nation" at www.T-Nation.com.

What you're about to read is about playing football, but the fact is it's about something much bigger. It's about dreams, and what it takes to make them come true.

Because everybody has dreams – dreams are easy. You don't even have to close your eyes to imagine yourself winning the Superbowl, or climbing Mount Everest, or finally buying Mom the house she always wanted.

But the road between dreams and reality is much harder. It's rarely short or without obstacles – it's usually a long and complicated path filled with enough setbacks and self-doubt that would make most turn back, siding with the naysayers who told them that their goal was "unrealistic" or "impractical," or "childish" or "stupid." Or just a dream.

Growing up in Illinois, I had one dream: to play Division I football. It wasn't the NFL – it was suiting up on Saturdays and playing for a big time school. I don't know when the dream started, but I can't tell you when it wasn't a goal of mine.

I punished my body for years in the weight room, on the track, and on the field all for one goal. I didn't ask too many questions with training; Walter Payton ran hills? Jim Wendler would run hills. Barry Sanders squatted? Jim Wendler would squat until his legs fell off. I did so without contemplating over-training (this didn't exist) or counting carbs. Asking questions felt like a waste of time, time that could be spent running and squatting.

Since then I've been through harder things, like divorce, children, and the death of loved ones. But at the time this was the biggest thing in my life, and the hardest. It's been over 15 years and I still look at those experiences and draw strength and wisdom from them.

When I went to the University of Arizona, I was two years removed from high school. I spent the first two years playing ball at the United States Air Force Academy (this was pre-tattoos and pre-beard) and realized that military life wasn't for me. I also realized that I needed to pursue what was in my heart.

So I left – literally packed one bag and flew to Tucson, Arizona without knowing a soul or having a guarantee that I was going to make the team. Below is what transpired and

(I hope) is a guide for the young players that have the same dream I once had.

CHOOSING YOUR SCHOOL

You may or may not have a choice of where you go to school. Financial and geographical restrictions may limit your choices to one or two. But if you have a choice, I highly recommend looking at schools with a good program for walk-ons.

While it may be easier to simply ask players for input, it isn't realistic. What I did was get the football media guides of each school and read the player bios. Saw which contributing players were walk-ons and who received scholarships. If possible, visit the schools and try to meet the recruiting coordinator (or any coach that will see you).

Assuming you have choices, choose the school that you feel most comfortable with. Remember that you will be a student, an athlete, and part of a community. This is a four or five year commitment on your part so make sure you're happy with your decision. Remember that your parents aren't going to the school, you are. So don't make a choice based on what they want.

If you don't have much of a choice, you're going to have to make the school and program work for you. You'll have to adjust and change your attitude to make your success.

THE TRYOUT

Unless you're a preferred walk-on, you'll have to go through a tryout. This involves a coach and some graduate assistant coaches taking you through a variety of drills and football specific stuff to see who can play. If you have a modicum of talent, preparedness, and speed, you'll be fine.

I've seen many players show up to these things out of shape and with a carefree attitude. This is a good thing, as it will allow you to shine. If they want to waste their opportunity of a lifetime, so be it. Show them up and shine.

Preparing for this is easy – be fast, strong, and in-shape. Don't take the summer off and fart around with high school friends that you won't care about in two years. That part of your life is done, and if they want to "go out with a bang," tell them you want to "go in with a fist of hate." People may see this as cold. I see this as part of achieving your greatness.

ATTITUDE

This can't be stressed enough – the one thing that's going to carry you through all the tough times as a walk-on (and in life) is your attitude. Every self-help guru has their own version of being a positive person; mantras to help you keep going through life and succeed.

I've always had a chip on my shoulder. I always feel that it's me against the world. I'm not good enough, strong enough, smart enough, or anything "enough" to adopt a happy-go-lucky attitude towards success. It's always a battle for me. This can be draining at times but this is how I can overcome obstacles – with a drive that I have something to prove and nothing to lose.

This may not be what gets you out of bed every morning, raring to tear life's head off. But whatever does get you out of bed, you have to harness it and live it. You know the saying, "Get knocked down seven times, but get up eight"? I prefer to get up eight times and knock out whoever knocked me down the first seven times.

Adopt a winning attitude that understands you will fail but allows you to achieve your goals.

If possible, have someone in your life that won't coddle you, but call you out on your fallacies. Whenever I faltered from this attitude my father set me straight.

1. Complained about school? Suck it up and study.

2. The coaches won't look at me? Quit crying and get better.

3. I don't like my job! Change your attitude or quit and do your own thing.

4. I don't make enough money! Find a way to make more.

People tell me I'm too blunt and "mean" when I answer training questions. Be happy it's not my father answering them.

THE BAD

Let's get this out of the way – being a walk-on at a major college sucks. One hundred percent of walk-ons were good or great high school football players and used to being the Big Fish. They got the cheerleaders, the press, and the notoriety that comes from being an athletic stand out in high school.

This all changes when you're a walk-on. If you're expecting any of the perks that you once had, you're in for a very rude awakening.

The coaches won't respect you, many of the players won't respect you, the strength coaches will look at you as a burden, and the equipment managers will hand you the worst equipment they have in hopes of driving you out of their office. I've been handed cleats that I wouldn't have worn in Pee Wee football – heavy, molded high tops that had more in common with Herman Munster than Tom Rathman. I actually had to go out and buy cleats when I was in college.

I've heard what coaches say about walk-ons – some even had the decency to say it to my face. "You'll be lucky to see the field from the stands," and other gems of positive encouragement. I've heard strength coaches laugh and go back into their offices when walk-ons come into the weight room. I'm positive that few coaches will ever bother learning your name.

You might get a real number the first couple of years, but many times you and a fellow walk-on will have the same number. So there might be two number "34"'s on your team, neither with your name on the jersey.

While at Arizona, the walk-ons had a separate locker room. Old school cage lockers stuck inside a utility room/boiler room/storage room. When one of us got called up to the Big Locker Room, we were all happy for him (there's a huge sense of camaraderie amongst walk-ons), but we couldn't help but be a little jealous. If you weren't, you didn't have the right attitude.

There's an old saying, "Show me a good loser and I'll show you a loser." Instead of complaining about it and pouting, most of us put our heads down and worked harder – that's how you properly channel setbacks and challenges. You're either a man of action or a coward.

Remember that your role as a walk-on, especially in the beginning, is really nothing more than a tackling dummy. And your job can literally be taken by a "dummy," a large foam bag covered in vinyl that has handles for the coach to hold.

You'll run countless plays, the same plays, repeatedly, and your body will be bruised, battered, and your head will ring. All so your teammates get a "good look" at the opposing teams plays and formations.

You think a 250-pound linebacker hits hard? Wait until his coach berates him endlessly and said linebacker knows exactly where the play is going.

And when practice is over, the rest of the team goes for the Team Meal while you trek back to your room for ramen noodles and RC Cola. You couldn't feel less a part of the team at this point. But that's the way the world works, and something very valuable I learned from all this is that you don't get treated fairly, nor should you.

The idea of fairness is a ridiculous notion – if you have something to offer then you should be treated as such. If you're a scrub in life, don't expect to be treated like someone that has value.

If the star of the team – the guy that makes the plays and makes the team go – is late to a meeting, it's brushed off. If you, the scrub tackling dummy, are late, you'll get booted out of the meeting and you'll be running after practice (that is if they care enough to stay late and waste their time with you).

There are two kinds of people in the world: the ones that protest and complain and want fairness despite never having earned it, and the ones that fight their butts off to be important and make a contribution. You have to earn the right to be treated fair. The people that have a problem with that are the scrubs. If you take one thing from this article, let that be it.

TAKE ADVANTAGE OF YOUR OPPORTUNITIES

As a walk-on you have few opportunities. So you'd better take advantage of the few that you get. You'd better be physically and mentally ready. The physical part is easy – just train. Any idiot can run and lift.

But you better know the plays and know your assignment. Nothing annoys a coach more than a mental error. So while you may get frustrated and not bother with the playbook, being ignorant of the plays will get you in the doghouse quicker than crap through a goose.

At Arizona we had a Scout Bowl every Thursday. While the rest of the team had a light, half-pad walk through, the scrubs played in a controlled scrimmage. This was the one way that many of us had to showcase our skills.

However, there are a lot of scrubs and a lot of redshirt scholarship players, and the latter will always get playing time in the Scout Bowl. So even in your own game you may not even get to play.

One Thursday I got my opportunity. The redshirt scholarship players showed some prima donna attitude and didn't want to participate. Coach Dino Babers looked at me, asked me if I was ready and put me to work.

The good/bad thing about Scout Bowls is that the offense is run heavy – it's hard to get the passing game down when the receivers and quarterbacks don't practice together. There's no timing and these two positions need to have some practice time to get this down.

So while this is a good thing for a running back (more carries), it also allows the defense to stack the box and stuff the run. I must've carried the ball 20 times in a row with varying levels of success and I was dead tired. My head was cut open, my eyes stinging with blood and sweat, my nose busted, but there was no way I was ever coming out. I knew this was my one opportunity. This was it.

After that Thursday, I played in every single Saturday game. That was my opportunity. I had no idea it was coming when I woke up that Thursday morning, but if I hadn't showed up to play I probably would've never seen the field. The coaches saw something in me that day and my life changed.

As a walk-on, you'll have to find your own "Scout Bowl" moment – the time when you're called out to do something, anything. If you waste it and squander it by not being ready, that's your own fault. So be prepared.

KNOW YOUR ROLE

For many, this is going to be a hard pill to swallow. In high school, I was the starting tailback and outside linebacker. I never came out of the game. I ran with abandon and averaged over 100 yards a game on fewer carries than any running back. I ran hard and through people.

When I got to Arizona I had to come to grips that I was not going to play that role. I had to contribute wherever I was needed. Since I was slow, I had to gain some weight and play fullback. And this was in an offensive system that didn't use two backs frequently.

So put your ego aside and know that your role as a football player may change. You're going to have to be fluid – you may have to learn a new position if you want to get on the field. It may be a position that doesn't get the playing time or the glory that you're used to.

The important thing is that you make yourself indispensable at what you do. Work as hard as you can to be the best at your given role. If that's protecting the punter, do so with such precision that no one can take your job. Do not take your job for granted. Make it hard on the coaches to take you out. Do your job better than anyone.

THE GOOD

Despite all the adversity and hardships you go through, in the end, the good always outweighs the bad. There's nothing more satisfying than running onto that field after years of work. The people in the stands have no idea what you've gone through to get there. You're just a guy in pads, identity shrouded by a facemask and a number.

Who cares? Most don't know what it's like to dream your entire childhood for a single moment, then work thousands of hours through endless setbacks just to see it happen.

Some people might see it as luck (and there is some involved), but what they don't see, nor do they ever want to see, is the blood, sweat, pain, and early mornings that you persevered.

They don't want to see it simply because they don't want to know that their failures in life stem from not wanting to deal with being uncomfortable, taking a chance, failing time after time, and putting it all on the line.

I'm going to brag a bit here and I don't care. I had two defining moments in my college career, two things that I'll never forget.

My first carry ever went for a touchdown on ESPN. It was a Thursday night Game of the Week on ESPN. This was the only game being played that day. We were playing San Diego State in San Diego.

I believe it was the second quarter and we were on the 5-yard line. Keith Smith, the quarterback, got the call and looked at me. "Are you ready?" The call was "5-2," a simple fullback dive. The only thing I remember is diving into the end zone, jumping up and looking around for the ref's signal.

After seeing his two arms raised I began celebrating. And celebrating. And jumping, and more celebrating, so much so that the ref came over and threatened to flag me for excessive celebration.

Didn't matter – this was real and genuine. I sprinted off the field and was greeted by Keith Smith, who jumped and hugged me and I about took his arm off giving him a "high five."

It wasn't about the six points. It was the work to get there and the happiness that my close teammates felt. After the television break, I got the sideline camera and did the obligatory "Hi Mom and Dad!" even though they were at the game, and thanked my girlfriend at the time, and my dog, Betty. Yeah, I thanked my dog on national TV – just because no one else did. No one understood it except the friends who were watching and they laughed because they knew how ridiculous it was.

The next day, I walked in the weight room to lift and the whole staff started clapping and hugging me. These were the people I'd spent countless hours with and with whom I had a great bond. Seeing them so happy was amazing.

That weekend, my good friend Matt Rhodes (also a walk-on) threw me a huge party at his sister's apartment complex.

There were tons of people and drinks and Matt kept introducing me, "This is Jim Wendler. He's a star football player and scores touchdowns. You might want to know him."

My second defining moment came at the end of training camp, when scholarships for walk-ons are announced. This was a big deal for us, and it's not about the money. It's about the respect of the coaches and players. You can always make money but you have to work to earn respect.

When the head coach, Dick Tomey, announced my name at the end of Two-a-Days my senior year, I cried like a little girl. I ran back and called my parents and cried in the phone. I thought about all the injuries. The critics. The years lifting and running. Every second was worth it. This was something I earned through years of work. No one could take it away.

THE END

Before every game, coaches, family and friends send you onto the field with good luck wishes. The truth is, luck will not make you run faster, hit harder or throw further. For that matter, luck will have little to do with succeeding in any of life's endeavors. Consider yourself lucky if you have gumption. Consider yourself lucky if you have strong determination. Consider yourself lucky if you believe in yourself. Create your own luck. Luck favors the most physical and highly committed individuals and teams. It has been said that luck is a place where preparation and opportunity come together. Follow the suggestions of this book so you can be successfully recruited and continue your athletic career. I would wish you Good luck in the pursuit of your endeavors but you don't need it. So I say...

Good courage, good skill, and good preparation!

ADVICE FROM TIM BROWN

EVERYONE HAS A PLAN UNTIL THEY GET HIT, AND OTHER LESSONS.

Football is a game of inches. Often in football, a few inches can swing momentum in a game, or be the difference in winning and losing. Its hard to believe that an entire athletic contest can be determined by such a minute measure, that men have wrestled for control, sweating and exerting themselves, only to have a basic unit of measurement determine the outcome of all their effort.

Life is much like that. It's hard to believe how marginal the difference is between a set of outcomes can be for us. Sometimes we are just lucky to have been the X person standing in line. Or, on a more serious note, shooting victims miss dying by inches. Whether it be receiving a promotion or missing a traffic light, this corollary applies.

Run to the ball and good things happen. Running to the ball in football is sound advice since everything revolves around the ball. A team cannot score without the ball; a team needs to advance the ball utilizing its personnel. So, in order to be able to make an impact, one needs to be around the ball.

The same thing goes in life. Find out where the action is and gravitate toward it. You will likely receive some of the positive benefits of being in the vicinity.

Everyone has a plan until they get hit. Though I've never played running back (I was a lineman), I'm sure they all think the same way: they are going to get the ball, juke left, outrun the defenders, score a touchdown, and get the cheerleader's phone number. Then they get the hand off and there's a huge middle linebacker who plants them on their back, causing them to re-evaluate why they decided to play ball in the first place.

In life, we like to plan everything out and feel like we know how it will turn out. That is, until we face a little adversity. Then we get to find out what our true character is. Do we regroup and move forward? Or do we fold it in? Were our plans even that important to begin with?

Give 110% on every play to the echo of the whistle. This trope is clichéd in society such that everyone recognizes what it means. Give full effort when you are involved in the play. This means that everything you do, do to the best of your ability. This will reduce your chance of injury and much like running to the ball, good things happen. And if you continue to give good effort until the very end (play until the echo of the whistle), then you will be in a position to benefit from something good, or at the very least, have no regrets about the outcome. If we took the same approach to life, there would be a lot less people carrying regret and sorrow because they gave their best at the initial opportunity.

Don't complain to the referees. This is pretty self-explanatory. The referees are there to enforce the rules, or are the personification of the rulebook. You can argue with them until you are blue in the face, but it won't change the call. Its best to go back to the huddle, regroup, and give a better effort the next time.

Life's the same way ... you will be dealt a hand that you had no control over how it was dealt to you. Maybe you are an orphan, or your family was poor, or maybe you were middle class looking at the rich kids across the street. That sucks, but that's life. You do have control over your approach in pursuing your success.

You have to want it more. At the end of the day, the attitude and effort we give on the football field determined our wins and losses most of the time. We were able to beat teams that were more talented because we outworked them consistently over the course of a game. There were games that we lost to supremely talented guys, but we could live with that; we maximized our abilities and though the other team was victorious, it did not come easy.

That's what life is about in a nutshell: perseverance. There may be things that we want today that we may not have. But we cannot give up; we must press forward and endure. We have to continue to have ambition and drive to strive. Our prior circumstances only provide us with challenges for our next steps.

Of course, football taught me much more than I have laid out here. I thank the game for the wonderful messages inscribed in the subtlety of each snap. When my children grow up, hopefully they will have a chance to play football and learn lessons within a relatively safe and structured context, as opposed to the hard knocks of real life.

APPENDIX 2

VALIDITY CONFIRMED: INFORMATION YOU CAN USE AS GIVEN TO US BY FRANK GANSZ

This section is dedicated to the memory of Frank Gansz. Considered perhaps the top special teams coach in the history of the NFL. Gansz twice earned special teams coach of the year honors, including 1999 when helped the St. Louis Rams to a Super Bowl victory. Gansz was a veteran of 38 seasons of coaching - 24 in the NFL and 14 in the collegiate ranks. It is an honor to have played for Coach Gansz at SMU for 14 months before he passed away on April 27, 2009 from complications following knee replacement surgery.

SMU Head Football Coach and former National Coach of the Year, June Jones:

"During one's lifetime there will be 4-5 people that impact you in your lifetime. They will change you. They will develop you into the person that you become. Frank Gansz was one of those people for me. He also was that person for all those that he coached, and for those who worked together with him.

There was no greater man that I have met in my lifetime than Frank Gansz. He taught us history, how to study, how to be a better husband, better father, better teammate, how to sacrifice, how to give, how to persevere, how to love, how to be the best we could possible be. We learned not only how to win football games, but how to win in life.

I had the privilege to be around Frank for almost 40 years. We worked together and were best friends for the last 20 years of his lifetime. What you are about to read will be with us all forever. I hope this information will live on with all of you so that the man that "Left Yesterday" will never be forgotten."

—

One of Frank Gansz' favorite sayings was, "What we give will grow. What we keep we lose." The following is a summary of notes pertaining to life and football, which were taken from team meetings led by Coach Gansz while at SMU from 2008-2009.

HIGH PERFORMANCE BUSINESS

"If you are going to fight in the North Atlantic, you have to train in the North Atlantic."
– *Admiral Ernest J. King*

You must play the game at the highest level to be the best.

How: The freedom to play the game at the highest level is earned on the practice field. Tough, specific, unreasonable, commitments! High standards.

- Establish standards. Hold yourself to those standards.

You can expect to play at your highest level when you have the highest standards of preparation and those standards are being met!

In order to play the game at its highest level, you must be able to attack problems.

What is a problem?

- A problem is anything that keeps you from performing at your highest level.

You must be able to confirm validity.

- What you say and do must be the same.

The greater the pressure, the higher the degree of difficulty. The more ominous the danger, the greater the need for teamwork!

- Gung Ho – work together in harmony

- Espirit de corps – a common spirit of comradeship, enthusiasm, and devotion to a cause among the members of a group

DON'T LET THE OTHER GUY DOWN

"What we have done for ourselves dies with us, what we have done for others and the world remains, and is immortal!"
– *Albert Pines*

Develop powerful lines of communication. I need to be able to tell you what I need from you to perform at my highest level. And you need to be able to tell me what you need from me to perform at your highest level.

Four types of communication:

1. Phatic – Small talk, "How are you."

2. Cathartic – Moaners, complainers, and negativity. This will weigh you down.

3. Persuasive – Being influenced by another's opinion. Can be positive or negative.

4. Informative – This is the <u>key</u>. Information you can use.

Manage your thought process. Learn to maintain a running mental dialogue with yourself. Talk kindly to yourself. Avoid being negative. Also, keep a daily journal; collect only information you can use.

STRIVE TO BE SUCCESSFUL

"The achievement of your goal is assured
the moment you commit yourself to it."
- *Matt Douglas*

Three things to be successful on the field:

1. Attitude

2. Effort

3. Ability

NO LIMITS

In order to have no limits, you need:

- Training (Practice)

- Opportunity (Games)

What you have to do:

- Step by step progression

- Painstaking attention to detail

- Must be able to confirm validity at all times

- Build on your success

- Study the heroic

These things will put you in touch with the greatness within you.

Always put the team first

- Team success is a prerequisite to personal success.

Do something heroic.

WHAT IS A HERO?

A person who, when <u>tested</u>, excels and, in doing so, inspires others to greatness.

Nurture your mind with great thoughts.

- To believe in the heroic makes heroes.

HABITS

"We are what we repeatedly do.
Excellence then is not an act but a habit."
- Aristotle

To be your best, you need to develop daily habits.

- Tough, specific, unreasonable, commitments! (HIGH STANDARDS).

- Must have ongoing technique and skill development.

- Get to your technique faster; play with better leverage than your opponent.

- Gain the advantage in the critical moments when man measures man.

- Run full speed to balance, with full body control and coordination.

- Take the initiative and responsibility to make things happen.

- The future belongs to those who make things happen.

- Live up to your objective, manage your behavior, and let nothing get in your way.

MENTAL TOUGHNESS

> "Great men are just ordinary men
> with extraordinary determination."
> - *Disraeli*

Mental Toughness: The ability to withstand pressure and failure and keep coming back until you succeed. To rise above hardship and disappointment until you succeed.

As an athlete competing at the highest level, once you experience something (confirmed performance) you automatically raise your expectations.

The Zone: Playing with no concern about the result. No Fear, No Worry, No Uncertainty, No Limits!

Champions and Championship Teams are *ACDC*

- More Aggressive

- More Confident

- More Disciplined

- Better Communicators

Five phases you must know and execute to be successful on game day:

1. Alignment

2. Assignment

3. Technique

4. Execution

5. Finish

DISCIPLINE

> "And the job demanded more;
> it demanded all you have and more."
> – *Mark Bowden, Black Hawk Down*

Football demands you to be disciplined. There is also a valuable life lesson in the scrutiny and evaluation process. From high school on up, coaches and fellow players through film will evaluate every move in practice and games. This is like life, where if we hope to improve and grow, we have to take responsibility for that growth.

Frank V. Gansz
November 22, 1938 – April 27, 2009

ABOUT THE AUTHOR

Mickey Dollens played defensive line for the Southern Methodist University football team, where he earned a full-ride scholarship (2006). Mickey graduated with a B.A. in English and a minor in psychology, before focusing his efforts on joining the U.S. Bobsled team, competing on the America's Cup tour. Outside of his athletics and writing careers, Dollens is the owner and developer of the Dallas-based longboarding company, Hilltop Boards. Mickey Dollens continues to pursue wide and varied interests. For further information, please visit his website www.MickeyDollens.com.

NOTES

NOTES

NOTES

NOTES

CPSIA information can be obtained at www.ICGtesting.com
Printed in the USA
LVOW12s2023130913

352214LV00002B/89/P